THE HEALING ARTS OF INDIA

AN EXPLORATION OF AYURVEDA, YOGA, AND NATUROPATHY

DR. JAGADEESH PILLAI

Made with ♥ on the Notion Press Platform
www.notionpress.com

|| Dedicated to Wisdom Seekers Around The World ||

Contents

Contents

Prayer

**"Om Poornamadah Poornamidam Poornat
Poornamudachyate,Poornasya Poornamaadaya
Poornamevavashishyate,Om Shantih, Shantih, Shantih"**

*The literal interpretation of this mantra is: That which is
Absolute, This which is Absolute, Absolute arises from Absolute,
If Absolute is removed from Absolute, Absolute remains
OM Peace, Peace, Peace.*

ᘧᘧᘧ

About The Author

Dr. Jagadeesh Pillai is a renowned Guinness World Record holder, writer, and researcher hailing from Varanasi, also known as the abode of Lord Shiva. With a Ph.D. in Vedic Science and a range of creative ideas and achievements, he is a true polymath. He is the author of more than 100 books including Research Publications. Although his roots can be traced back to Kerala, the people of Varanasi hold him in high regard and affectionately consider him one of their own.

Dr. Pillai has achieved four Guinness World Records in the following subjects:

"Script to Screen" - In this record, Dr. Pillai produced and directed an animation film within the shortest time possible, breaking the previous record set by Canadians. He has also received numerous national and international awards and recognitions for this achievement.

Longest Line of Postcards - For this record, Dr. Pillai created a line of 16,300 postcards on the occasion of the 163rd anniversary of Indian Postal Day. The event also included a questionnaire about the Indian flag.

Largest Poster Awareness Campaign - Dr. Pillai designed an awareness campaign on the subject of "Beti Bachao - Beti Padhao" (Save the Girl Child - Educate the Girl Child) to achieve this record.

Largest Envelope - In tribute to the Indian Prime Minister's

"Make in India" initiative, Dr. Pillai created a 4000 square meter envelope using waste paper to achieve this record.

Attempted - **70000 Candles on a 210 kg Cake** - To celebrate the 70th Indian Independence Day, Dr. Pillai attempted to light 70,000 candles on a 210 kg cake, which was recorded in World Records India.

Attempted - **Documentary on Dhamek Stupa of Sarnath in 17 Languages** - Dr. Pillai attempted to create a documentary on the Dhamek Stupa of Sarnath, dubbing it in 17 different languages. The result of this attempt is currently awaiting confirmation from the Guinness World Records.

Dr. Pillai is skilled in teaching the Bhagavad Gita, a Hindu scripture, and is popular among young people. He has helped many young people improve their lives through his motivational teachings.

In addition to teaching, he has composed and sung numerous Sanskrit Bhajans and patriotic songs.

He has also written and directed several short films and documentaries for awareness campaigns, and has volunteered with the police in both UP and Kerala to spread awareness about various issues through videos and photography.

Incredibly, he has produced and directed over 100 documentaries about the city of Varanasi, all on his own.

He has also helped and guided more than 25 boys and girls to achieve world records through creative and innovative methods. He is a multifaceted person who uses his intellect and the blessings given to him by God to excel in various areas. He is both a teacher and a student, always learning and teaching, and is able to master any subject he comes across.

He is a selfless social activist and motivational speaker who has overcome struggles and failures to become a successful and enthusiastic individual with a rich life experience.

In addition to his work with the Bhagavad Gita, he is also an efficient Tarot card reader, Astro-Vastu consultant, and a talented singer and composer. He has sung the entire Ram Charita Manas and Bhagavad Gita in his own compositions, and has sung the phrase "Lokah Samastha Sukhino Bhavantu" in 50 different languages. He is currently working on a detailed and scientific study of Vedas, Upanishads, Puranas, and the Bhagavad Gita. He has also composed and sung the Hanuman Chalisa and Gayatri Mantra in 108 and 1008 different compositions, respectively.

Awards - Four Times Guinness World Records, Winner of Mahatma Gandhi Vishwa Shanti Puraskar, Mahatma Gandhi Global Peace Ambassador, Kashi Ratna Award, Dr. APJ Abdul Kalam Motivational Person of the Year 2017, Mother Teresa Award, Indira Gandhi Priyadarshini Award, Bharat Vikas Ratna Award, Udyog Ratna Award, Vigyan Prasar Award, Poorvanchal Ratn Samman.

❧❧❧

Preface

The Healing Arts of India: An Exploration of Ayurveda, Yoga, and Naturopathy is a comprehensive guide to the ancient healing systems of India. This book delves into the history, philosophy, and practices of Ayurveda, Yoga, and Naturopathy, and explores how these traditional healing systems can be used in the modern world to promote health and well-being.

The book begins with an introduction to the traditional healing systems of India, including a brief history and an overview of the key principles and practices of each system. It then goes on to explore the various aspects of Ayurveda, including its history, philosophy, diagnosis and treatment methods, and the use of herbal medicine.

The book also covers the science of yoga and its physical and mental benefits, as well as the tradition of naturopathy in India and its focus on diet and lifestyle for health and healing. Additionally, the book explores the lesser-known practices of Marma therapy and Panchakarma, and how yoga and Ayurveda can be used together for a holistic approach to health.

In this book, we also discuss the role of Yoga therapy and Ayurvedic herbology and pharmacology. As well as the importance of understanding Ayurveda and Cancer and the future of Indian traditional healing systems in modern world.

This book is intended for anyone interested in learning

more about the ancient healing systems of India and how they can be used to promote health and well-being in the modern world. It is also an invaluable resource for practitioners of Ayurveda, Yoga, and Naturopathy, as well as for healthcare professionals looking to integrate these traditional healing systems into their practice.

We hope that this book will inspire you to learn more about these ancient healing systems and to explore the many ways in which they can be used to promote health and well-being in your own life.

ᗞᗞᗞ

Disclaimer

"The information provided in this book related to Yoga and Ayurveda is for reference purposes only. It is not intended to be a substitute for professional medical advice, diagnosis, or treatment. Always seek the advice of a qualified healthcare provider with any questions you may have regarding a medical condition. The author and publisher of this book do not accept any responsibility for any errors or omissions or for any actions taken in reliance thereon. Any treatment or practice mentioned in this book should be done only under the guidance and supervision of a professional medical practitioner."

ONE

TRADITIONAL HEALING SYSTEMS OF INDIA

India has a rich history of traditional healing systems, with Ayurveda, Yoga, and Naturopathy being some of the most well-known and widely practiced. These ancient practices have been passed down through generations and continue to be an important part of India's healthcare system today. In this chapter, we will explore the origins and principles of these traditional healing systems and how they are used to promote health and wellness.

Ayurveda is one of the oldest medical systems in the world, with roots dating back to ancient India. It is based on the principle that good health is achieved by maintaining balance in the body, mind, and spirit. Ayurveda practitioners use a combination of herbal remedies, dietary changes, and lifestyle modifications to promote balance and prevent disease.

Yoga, which originated in India over 5,000 years ago, is a system of physical and mental practices that aim to unite the mind, body, and spirit. Yoga poses, or asanas, are designed to improve flexibility and strength, while meditation and breathing techniques are used to reduce stress and promote relaxation.

Naturopathy, also known as naturopathic medicine, is a holistic approach to healthcare that emphasizes the use of natural remedies and the body's own healing abilities. Naturopathic practitioners use a variety of therapies, such as herbal medicine, acupuncture, and massage, to treat a wide range of conditions and promote overall health and wellness.

Ayurveda, Yoga, and Naturopathy are traditional healing systems that have been practiced in India for thousands of years. They are based on the principles of balance and harmony, and aim to promote health and wellness through natural remedies, lifestyle changes, and physical and mental practices. Understanding these traditional healing systems can provide valuable insights into the holistic approach to healthcare that is deeply ingrained in Indian culture.

ᠵᠵᠵ

"Ayurveda is the sister science of yoga." - Dr. Robert Svoboda

TWO

THE HISTORY AND PHILOSOPHY OF AYURVEDA

Ayurveda is one of the oldest medical systems in the world, with roots dating back to ancient India. The name "Ayurveda" is derived from the Sanskrit words "ayus," meaning life, and "veda," meaning knowledge or science. The origins of Ayurveda can be traced back to the Vedic period of ancient India, around 3000 BCE, where it was initially passed down orally from master to student. The principles of Ayurveda were later documented in the ancient texts known as the Charaka Samhita and Sushruta Samhita, which are considered to be the foundation of Ayurvedic medicine.

The philosophy of Ayurveda is based on the belief that good health is achieved by maintaining balance in the body, mind, and spirit. According to Ayurveda, the universe is made up of five elements: earth, water, fire, air, and ether.

These elements are also present in the human body, and are represented by three fundamental energies, or doshas, called vata, pitta, and kapha. The doshas are responsible for maintaining balance in the body, and when they are in harmony, a person is considered to be in good health.

Ayurveda practitioners believe that illness and disease occur when the doshas become imbalanced. The practitioner will identify the dosha that is imbalanced and recommend treatment to restore balance. Treatment methods may include herbal remedies, dietary changes, and lifestyle modifications. Ayurveda also emphasizes the importance of preventative medicine, and encourages individuals to adopt healthy habits to maintain balance and prevent disease.

Ayurveda is not only a medical system, but also a way of life, it aims to promote overall well-being and balance in all aspects of life. It also encourages the use of mindfulness and self-awareness to understand the connection between the mind and body and how to maintain balance.

Ayurveda is an ancient healing system that has been passed down through generations in India. It is based on the principles of balance and harmony, and aims to promote health and wellness through the use of natural remedies, lifestyle changes, and a holistic approach that addresses the body, mind, and spirit.

ᏧᏧᏧ

"Yoga is the science to be in the here and now."
- Osho

THREE

AYURVEDIC DIAGNOSIS AND TREATMENT METHODS

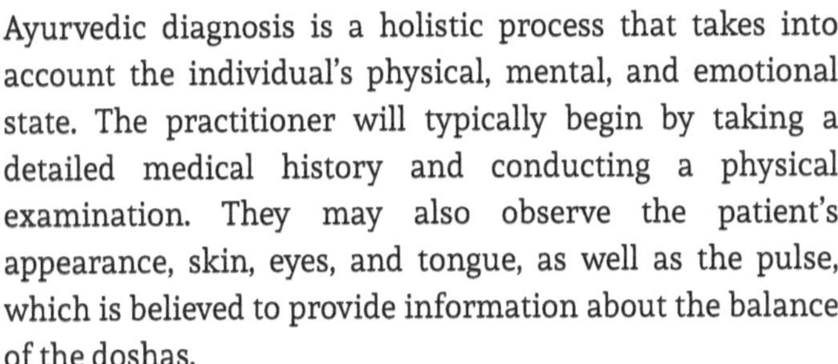

Ayurvedic diagnosis is a holistic process that takes into account the individual's physical, mental, and emotional state. The practitioner will typically begin by taking a detailed medical history and conducting a physical examination. They may also observe the patient's appearance, skin, eyes, and tongue, as well as the pulse, which is believed to provide information about the balance of the doshas.

In Ayurveda, diagnosis is based on the concept of tridosha, which states that each person has a unique balance of three doshas: vata, pitta, and kapha. Imbalances in these doshas are believed to be the underlying cause of illness and disease. The practitioner will use their knowledge of

Ayurvedic principles to determine which dosha or doshas are out of balance and the extent of the imbalance.

Ayurvedic treatment methods aim to restore balance to the doshas and promote overall health and well-being. Treatment methods may include:

Herbal remedies: Ayurveda uses a wide range of herbal medicines, including single herbs and herbal formulations, to address specific health conditions.

Dietary changes: Ayurveda practitioners may recommend changes to the patient's diet to balance the doshas.

Lifestyle modifications: Ayurveda encourages individuals to adopt healthy habits, such as regular exercise, yoga, and meditation, to maintain balance and prevent disease.

Panchakarma: Panchakarma is a five-fold therapeutic process that includes herbal oil massages, steam therapy, and the use of herbal enemas, which are believed to help detoxify the body and restore balance to the doshas.

Yoga and meditation: These are also important aspect of Ayurvedic treatment, as they help to balance the mind and body and promote overall health and well-being.

It is important to note that Ayurvedic treatment is tailored to the individual, based on their unique needs and health status. The practitioner will work with the patient to develop a treatment plan that takes into account the patient's specific health concerns and goals.

Ayurvedic diagnosis and treatment methods are based on the principles of balance and harmony, and aim to promote overall health and well-being by restoring balance to the doshas. Ayurvedic treatment methods include a wide range of therapies, such as herbal remedies, dietary changes, and lifestyle modifications, as well as yoga and meditation, and Panchakarma. The practitioner will work with the patient to develop a treatment plan that is tailored to the individual's specific needs and goals.

"Yoga is the fountain of youth. You're only as young as your spine is flexible." - Bob Harper

FOUR

YOGA: A MIND-BODY PRACTICE FOR WELLNESS

Yoga is a system of physical and mental practices that originated in ancient India over 5,000 years ago. The word "yoga" comes from the Sanskrit word "yuj," which means to unite or join, and refers to the union of the individual self with the universal self. Yoga is often described as a holistic approach to health and wellness that aims to unite the mind, body, and spirit.

One of the most well-known aspects of yoga is the practice of yoga poses or asanas. These poses are designed to improve flexibility and strength and promote physical wellness. The practice of yoga also includes pranayama, or breathing techniques, which are believed to help regulate the breath and promote relaxation and stress reduction.

Yoga is also known for its mental and emotional benefits, such as reducing stress, anxiety, and depression. It is believed that yoga can help to balance the mind and emotions by promoting inner peace and self-awareness.

Yoga also includes the practice of meditation and mindfulness, which are believed to help individuals develop a deeper understanding of themselves and the world around them. Through the practice of yoga, individuals can become more aware of their thoughts and emotions and learn how to manage them effectively.

Yoga can be practiced by people of all ages and fitness levels, and can be adapted to suit different needs and abilities. There are various styles of yoga, such as Hatha, Vinyasa, and Ashtanga, which offer different levels of intensity and focus.

Yoga is a mind-body practice that originated in ancient India. It is a holistic approach to health and wellness that aims to unite the mind, body, and spirit. The practice of yoga includes the physical practice of yoga poses, breathing techniques, meditation, and mindfulness. Yoga is believed to have many physical and mental health benefits, such as reducing stress, anxiety and depression, promoting relaxation and inner peace, and can be practiced by people of all ages and fitness levels.

ᛩᛩᛩ

"Yoga is not about self-improvement, it's about self-acceptance." - Gurmukh Kaur Khalsa

FIVE

THE SCIENCE OF YOGA: PHYSICAL AND MENTAL BENEFITS

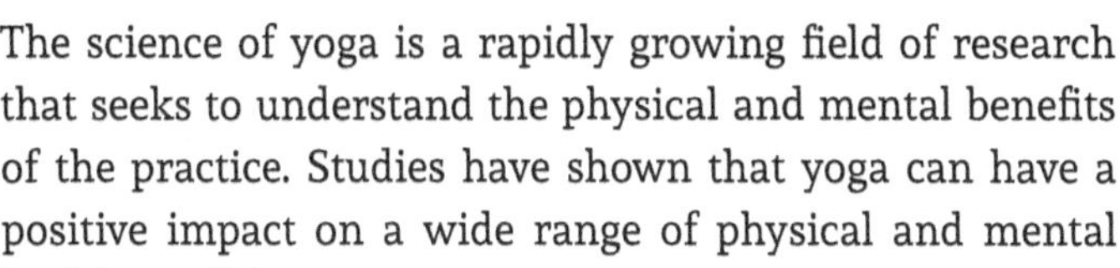

The science of yoga is a rapidly growing field of research that seeks to understand the physical and mental benefits of the practice. Studies have shown that yoga can have a positive impact on a wide range of physical and mental health conditions.

From a physical perspective, yoga has been shown to improve flexibility, strength, balance, and cardiovascular health. Yoga poses, or asanas, can help to stretch and tone muscles, improve posture and balance, and increase cardiovascular fitness. Additionally, yoga can also help to reduce chronic pain, improve respiratory function, and lower blood pressure.

Yoga's mental and emotional benefits are also well-documented. Yoga has been shown to reduce stress and anxiety by promoting relaxation and inner peace. It can also help to improve mood, reduce symptoms of depression, and increase feelings of well-being. Yoga's mindfulness and self-awareness practices can also help individuals to develop a deeper understanding of themselves and the world around them.

Yoga is also believed to have neuroprotective effects, which can help to protect the brain from damage caused by aging and disease. Research suggests that yoga may help to improve cognitive function, memory, and concentration.

It's worth noting that not all studies have found positive results for all the physical and mental health conditions. However, many studies have been done with small sample sizes, and more research is needed to confirm the results.

The science of yoga is a rapidly growing field of research that seeks to understand the physical and mental benefits of the practice. Studies have shown that yoga can have a positive impact on a wide range of physical and mental health conditions, including flexibility, strength, balance, cardiovascular health, stress, anxiety, depression, mood, well-being, cognitive function, memory, and concentration. However, more research is needed to confirm the results.

 මමම

"Yoga is the journey of the self, through the self, to the self." - Bhagavad Gita

SIX

THE TRADITION OF NATUROPATHY IN INDIA

Naturopathy, also known as naturopathic medicine, is a holistic approach to healthcare that emphasizes the use of natural remedies and the body's own healing abilities. Naturopathy originated in Germany in the late 19th century and was later introduced to India in the early 20th century. The tradition of naturopathy in India has been growing in popularity in recent years, as more people are looking for natural and alternative forms of healthcare.

Naturopathy in India is based on the belief that the body has the innate ability to heal itself, and that good health can be achieved by supporting and enhancing this natural healing process. Naturopathic practitioners use a variety of therapies, such as herbal medicine, acupuncture, and massage, to treat a wide range of conditions and promote overall health and wellness.

Naturopathy also emphasizes the importance of preventative medicine, and encourages individuals to adopt healthy habits, such as regular exercise, a balanced diet, and adequate rest, to maintain good health and prevent disease.

Naturopathic practitioners in India are trained in a variety of natural therapies, such as Ayurveda, Yoga, Acupuncture, Homeopathy, Unani and traditional Chinese medicine. Naturopathy is also integrated with modern diagnostic techniques and laboratory investigations to provide holistic care.

Naturopathy is a holistic approach to healthcare that emphasizes the use of natural remedies and the body's own healing abilities. Naturopathy tradition in India is growing in popularity and it is based on the belief that the body has the innate ability to heal itself, and that good health can be achieved by supporting and enhancing this natural healing process. Naturopathic practitioners use a variety of therapies, such as herbal medicine, acupuncture, and massage, to treat a wide range of conditions and promote overall health and wellness. Naturopathy also emphasizes the importance of preventative medicine and encourages individuals to adopt healthy habits to maintain good health and prevent disease.

ppp

"Yoga is the control of the modifications of the
mind." - Patanjali

SEVEN

NATUROPATHIC DIET AND HEALING

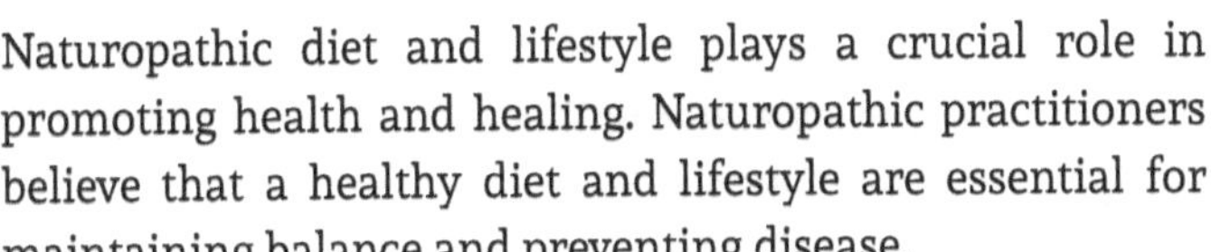

Naturopathic diet and lifestyle plays a crucial role in promoting health and healing. Naturopathic practitioners believe that a healthy diet and lifestyle are essential for maintaining balance and preventing disease.

A naturopathic diet is typically based on whole, unprocessed foods that are in season and locally grown. The diet emphasizes fresh fruits and vegetables, whole grains, and lean proteins, and minimizes the consumption of processed foods, sugar, and saturated fats. Naturopathic practitioners may also recommend specific dietary changes based on an individual's unique needs and health condition.

Naturopathic practitioners also believe that a healthy lifestyle is essential for maintaining balance and preventing disease. They may recommend regular exercise, adequate rest, and stress management techniques, such as yoga, meditation, or deep breathing. Naturopathic practitioners also emphasize the importance of exposure to nature and regular time outdoors to promote physical and emotional well-being.

Naturopathic practitioners also recommend to avoid exposure to toxins, such as pollutants, pesticides, and chemicals found in personal care products, cleaning supplies, and other household items. They may also recommend to use natural products instead of synthetic or chemical-based products.

Naturopathic practitioners also stress on the importance of regular check-ups and screenings to detect any potential health problems early and address them before they become serious. They also recommend regular self-care practices, such as regular self-massage and hydrotherapy, to promote overall health and well-being.

Naturopathic diet and lifestyle plays a crucial role in promoting health and healing. Naturopathic practitioners believe that a healthy diet, regular exercise, adequate rest, stress management techniques, exposure to nature, avoidance of toxins, regular check-ups and screenings, and regular self-care practices are essential for maintaining balance and preventing disease. Naturopathic practitioners may also recommend specific dietary changes based on an individual's unique needs and health condition.

ϷϷϷ

"The purpose of yoga is to create strength, awareness and harmony in both the mind and body." - B.K.S. Iyengar

EIGHT

MARMA THERAPY: AYURVEDIC ACUPUNCTURE

Marma therapy is an Ayurvedic form of acupuncture that involves the stimulation of specific points on the body called marmas. These points are believed to be connected to the body's vital energy, or prana, and are thought to have the ability to balance the body's doshas and promote overall health and well-being.

Marma therapy is based on the principle that the body is made up of 107 marma points, which are located at the intersection of muscles, bones, tendons, and ligaments. These points are thought to be connected to the body's vital organs and systems and are believed to have the ability to balance the body's doshas and promote overall health and well-being.

Marma therapy is typically performed by trained Ayurvedic

practitioners, who use a variety of techniques to stimulate the marma points, such as massage, pressure, and the use of herbal oils. The practitioner will determine which marma points need to be stimulated based on the individual's unique needs and health condition.

Marma therapy is believed to have a wide range of health benefits, such as reducing pain and inflammation, improving circulation, and promoting relaxation and stress reduction. It is also thought to help alleviate a variety of health conditions, such as arthritis, headaches, and respiratory problems.

It's worth noting that Marma therapy is not widely accepted by the scientific community and studies on its efficacy are limited. More research is needed to confirm the benefits of marma therapy and understand its mechanism of action.

Marma therapy is an Ayurvedic form of acupuncture that involves the stimulation of specific points on the body called marmas. These points are believed to be connected to the body's vital energy, or prana, and are thought to have the ability to balance the body's doshas and promote overall.

ᗞᗞᗞ

"Yoga is the practice of quieting the mind." - Patanjali

NINE

PANCHAKARMA: AYURVEDA'S DETOXIFICATION THERAPY

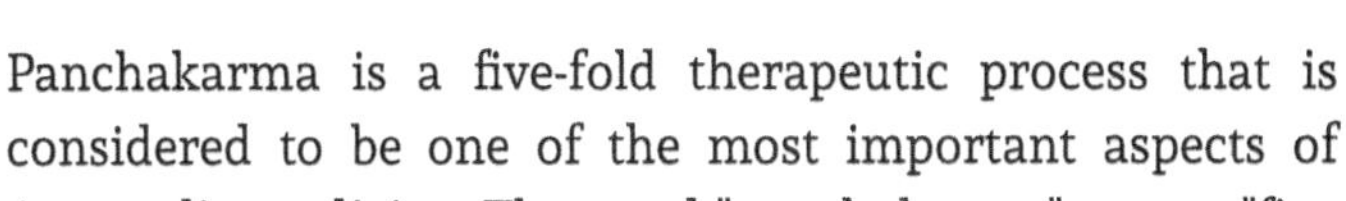

Panchakarma is a five-fold therapeutic process that is considered to be one of the most important aspects of Ayurvedic medicine. The word "panchakarma" means "five actions" in Sanskrit, and the five actions are:

Vamana: This is a process of therapeutic vomiting that is used to eliminate excess kapha from the body.

Virechana: This is a process of therapeutic purgation that is used to eliminate excess pitta from the body.

Basti: This is a process of enema therapy that is used to eliminate excess vata from the body.

Nasya: This is a process of nasal therapy that is used to cleanse and rejuvenate the head and neck region.

Raktamokshana: This is a process of bloodletting that is used to purify the blood and eliminate toxins.

Panchakarma is believed to help detoxify the body and restore balance to the doshas, which are the three fundamental principles of Ayurvedic medicine. The process is typically preceded by a period of preparatory procedures called purva karma, which includes snehana and swedana to loosen and mobilize the toxins from the tissues before the actual Panchakarma procedure.

Panchakarma is believed to have a wide range of health benefits, including reducing stress and tension, improving digestion, promoting a sense of well-being, and helping to prevent and treat a variety of health conditions.

It is important to note that Panchakarma should only be performed by trained and qualified Ayurvedic practitioners. The therapy should be tailored to an individual's specific needs and health condition, and it is also important to note that Panchakarma should not be used as a substitute for conventional medical treatment in serious or life-threatening conditions.

Panchakarma is a five-fold therapeutic process that is considered to be one of the most important aspects of Ayurvedic medicine.

ppp

"Yoga is the perfect balance of mind, body and spirit." - Ganga White

TEN

Yoga and Ayurveda: A Synergy for Health

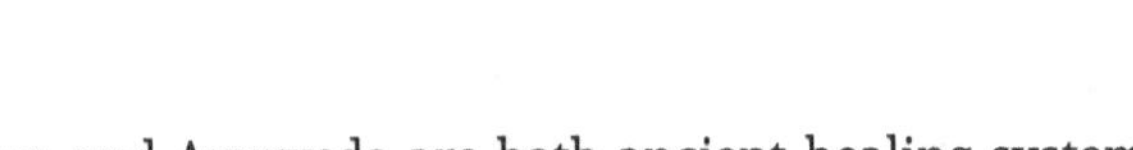

Yoga and Ayurveda are both ancient healing systems that originated in India and share many similarities. Both systems view health and well-being as a state of balance and harmony between the mind, body, and spirit.

Ayurveda is a holistic system of medicine that focuses on maintaining balance in the body's doshas, which are the three fundamental principles of Ayurvedic medicine. Yoga, on the other hand, is a system of physical and mental practices that aim to unite the mind, body, and spirit.

The practices of yoga and Ayurveda complement each other, as they both focus on promoting balance and harmony in the body. Yoga poses, or asanas, can help to stretch and tone muscles, improve posture, and increase flexibility and strength. This can help to balance the doshas and maintain physical health. Yoga's breathing techniques, or pranayama, can also help to regulate the breath and promote relaxation and stress reduction.

Ayurveda's use of herbal medicine, massage, and other natural therapies can also support the body's natural healing process. Ayurveda and Yoga together can help to promote overall health and well-being by addressing both the physical and mental aspects of an individual.

Additionally, both Yoga and Ayurveda focus on the importance of a healthy lifestyle, including regular exercise, a balanced diet, and adequate rest, to maintain good health and prevent disease.

Yoga and Ayurveda are both ancient healing systems that originated in India and share many similarities. Both systems view health and well-being as a state of balance and harmony between the mind, body, and spirit. The practices of yoga and Ayurveda complement each other, as they both focus on promoting balance and harmony in the body, and addressing both the physical and mental aspects of an individual. Both systems also focus on the importance of a healthy lifestyle to maintain good health and prevent disease.

ﻉﻉﻉ

"Yoga is the art work of awareness on the canvas of body, mind, and soul." - Amit Ray

ELEVEN

Yoga Therapy: A Holistic Healing

Yoga therapy is the use of yoga practices and principles to address specific health conditions and promote overall health and well-being. Yoga therapy is a holistic approach to healing that addresses the physical, mental, and emotional aspects of an individual.

Yoga therapy can be used to treat a wide range of health conditions, including chronic pain, stress, anxiety, depression, and high blood pressure. Yoga therapy can also be used to support recovery from injuries and surgeries, as well as to improve overall physical and mental function.

Yoga therapy typically involves the use of specific yoga poses, or asanas, that are tailored to an individual's specific needs and health condition. The therapist may also incorporate breathing techniques, or pranayama, and meditation to help promote relaxation and reduce stress. Yoga therapy may also include the use of props such as blankets, blocks, and straps to help the individual achieve proper alignment and support during the practice.

Yoga therapy is often provided by trained yoga therapists, who have completed specialized training in yoga therapy and have an understanding of the principles of anatomy, physiology and psychology. They may also work in collaboration with other healthcare providers such as physiotherapists and medical doctors.

Yoga therapy is believed to have a wide range of health benefits, including reducing stress and tension, improving digestion, promoting a sense of well-being, and helping to prevent and treat a variety of health conditions.

Yoga therapy is the use of yoga practices and principles to address specific health conditions and promote overall health and well-being. It is a holistic approach to healing that addresses the physical, mental, and emotional aspects of an individual. Yoga therapy typically involves the use of specific yoga poses, breathing techniques, and meditation, which are tailored to an individual's specific needs and health condition. Yoga therapy is often provided by trained yoga therapists and may be used to treat a wide range of health conditions, including chronic pain, stress, anxiety, depression, and high blood pressure. It is believed to have a wide range of health benefits and can be used in collaboration with other healthcare providers.

꧁꧂꧂

"Ayurveda is not a quick-fix. It's about creating balance in your life through food, lifestyle, and self-care practices." - Sahara Rose

TWELVE

AYURVEDIC HERBOLOGY AND PHARMACOLOGY

Ayurvedic herbology and pharmacology is the study of the medicinal properties of plants and their use in Ayurvedic medicine. Ayurveda is an ancient system of medicine that originated in India, and it has been used for thousands of years to diagnose, treat, and prevent a wide range of health conditions.

In Ayurveda, herbs are used to balance the doshas, which are the three fundamental principles of Ayurvedic medicine. Herbs are also used to support the body's natural healing processes, and to promote overall health and well-being.

Ayurvedic practitioners use a wide variety of herbs to treat a wide range of health conditions, including digestive disorders, respiratory problems, and skin conditions. Some of the most commonly used herbs in Ayurvedic medicine include turmeric, ginger, ashwagandha, and licorice.

Ayurvedic herbs are used in various forms, such as powders, decoctions, infusions, pastes, and oils. Ayurvedic practitioners may also use herbs in combination with other natural therapies such as massage, yoga, and meditation to achieve optimal results.

Ayurvedic herbology and pharmacology is a complex and vast field, and it requires extensive knowledge and training to practice safely and effectively. Ayurvedic practitioners are trained to understand the properties of different herbs and how to use them in a safe and effective manner. It's worth noting that Ayurvedic herbology and pharmacology have not been fully studied by the scientific community, and more research is needed to confirm the safety and efficacy of Ayurvedic herbal remedies.

Ayurvedic herbology and pharmacology is the study of the medicinal properties of plants and their use in Ayurvedic medicine. Ayurvedic practitioners use a wide variety of herbs to treat a wide range of health conditions and balance the doshas. Ayurvedic herbs are used in various forms such as powders, decoctions, infusions, pastes, and oils.

"Ayurveda is the science of life and the art of living." - Dr. Vasant Lad

THIRTEEN

YOGA AND MEDITATION FOR STRESS MANAGEMENT

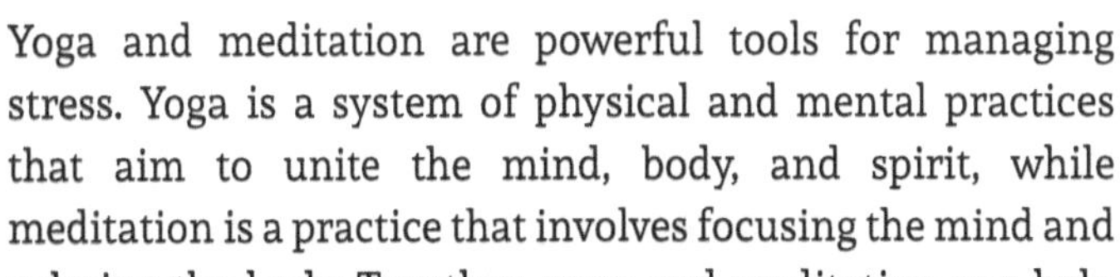

Yoga and meditation are powerful tools for managing stress. Yoga is a system of physical and mental practices that aim to unite the mind, body, and spirit, while meditation is a practice that involves focusing the mind and calming the body. Together, yoga and meditation can help to reduce stress and promote a sense of well-being.

Yoga practices, such as asanas (yoga poses), pranayama (breathing techniques), and relaxation techniques can help to decrease the physical symptoms of stress, such as tension in the muscles, shallow breathing, and increased heart rate. Yoga also helps to increase the flow of oxygen to the brain, which can help to improve mental clarity and concentration, and reduce feelings of anxiety and depression.

Meditation, on the other hand, can help to reduce the mental and emotional symptoms of stress, such as constant worrying, racing thoughts, and feelings of overwhelm. By focusing the mind and calming the body, meditation can help to reduce anxiety and promote feelings of peace and tranquility.

Yoga and meditation can also be used together to achieve a more profound and holistic stress management. The combination of physical and mental practices can help to reduce stress from different angles and provide a more complete stress management approach.

It's worth noting that Yoga and meditation should be practiced under the guidance of a qualified instructor and should not be used as a substitute for conventional medical treatment in serious or life-threatening conditions.

Yoga and meditation are powerful tools for managing stress. Yoga practices can help to decrease the physical symptoms of stress and improve mental clarity, while meditation can help to reduce the mental and emotional symptoms of stress. Together, yoga and meditation can provide a holistic approach to stress management and help to reduce feelings of anxiety and promote feelings of peace and tranquility.

ᗹᗹᗹ

"Ayurveda is not a system of healing, it's a way of living." - Dr. David Frawley

FOURTEEN

AYURVEDA AND CANCER

Ayurveda, an ancient Indian system of medicine, has a holistic approach to health, which includes the use of herbal medicines, dietary guidelines, and lifestyle recommendations. Some practitioners of Ayurveda believe that it can be used as an adjuvant therapy in cancer management, but it's important to note that Ayurveda alone cannot cure cancer.

Ayurveda practitioners may use herbal remedies to improve the patient's quality of life and reduce the side effects of cancer treatment, such as fatigue, pain, and nausea. They may also use dietary guidelines and lifestyle recommendations to support the patient's overall health and well-being.

It's worth noting that there is limited scientific evidence to support the use of Ayurveda in the treatment of cancer, and more research is needed to understand its potential effectiveness. Additionally, it's important to consult with a qualified healthcare professional before using Ayurvedic treatments, as they may interact with conventional cancer treatments.

It's also important to note that cancer is a serious condition and requires proper diagnosis and treatment by a qualified medical professional. Patients should not use Ayurveda as a substitute for conventional cancer treatments such as surgery, radiation, and chemotherapy. It's essential to work with a qualified healthcare professional who can provide guidance on the best approach for cancer treatment.

Ayurveda, an ancient Indian system of medicine, has a holistic approach to health and may be used as an adjuvant therapy in cancer management. Ayurveda practitioners may use herbal remedies, dietary guidelines, and lifestyle recommendations to improve the patient's quality of life and reduce the side effects of cancer treatment.

ϷϷϷ

"Yoga is the perfect opportunity to be curious about who you are." - Jason Crandell

FIFTEEN

THE FUTURE TRADITIONAL HEALING IN MODERN WORLD.

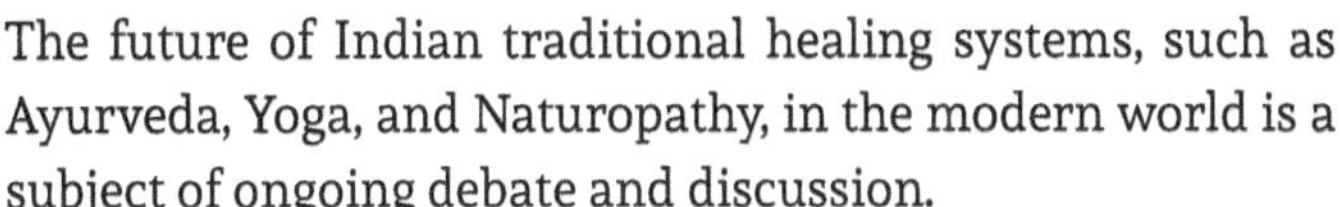

The future of Indian traditional healing systems, such as Ayurveda, Yoga, and Naturopathy, in the modern world is a subject of ongoing debate and discussion.

On one hand, there is increasing interest in these ancient healing systems as more people seek out natural and holistic approaches to health and wellness. This has led to a growing acceptance of these traditional healing systems in mainstream healthcare and a rise in the number of practitioners trained in these systems.

On the other hand, the lack of scientific evidence to support many of the claims made by practitioners of these traditional systems, and the absence of standardization of training and practice, can make it difficult for them to be fully integrated into modern healthcare.

However, there is a growing recognition of the importance of integrating traditional healing systems into modern healthcare. This includes the integration of Ayurvedic principles into modern medical practices, the use of yoga as a complementary therapy for a range of conditions, and the use of naturopathic practices in primary care.

Research is also underway to better understand the mechanisms of action of these traditional healing systems, and to develop evidence-based guidelines for their use. This will help to establish the effectiveness and safety of these systems, and increase their acceptance in modern healthcare.

The future of Indian traditional healing systems in the modern world is a complex and multifaceted issue. While there is increasing interest in these ancient healing systems, the lack of scientific evidence and the absence of standardization of training and practice can make it difficult for them to be fully integrated into modern healthcare. However, there is a growing recognition of the importance of integrating traditional healing systems into modern healthcare, and research is underway to better understand their mechanisms of action and develop evidence-based guidelines for their use.

ppp

Other Books Of The Author

1. The Moments When I Met God
2. Kashiyile Theertha Pathangal
3. GURU GYAN VANI
4. Abhiprerak Gita
5. ASSI SE JAIN GHAT TAK
6. Hopelessness of Arjuna
7. The Soul and It's True Nature
8. Sense of Action (Karma)
9. Action through Wisdom
10. Action through Wisdom
11. THEORY AND PRACTICAL OF EVERY ACTION
12. LOGICAL UNDERSTANDING OF THE SUPREME
13. THE IMPERISHABLE SUPREME
14. Yatra Nishadraj se Hanuman Ghat Tak
15. Yatra Karnatak Ghat se Raja Ghat Tak
16. Yatra Pandey Ghat se Prayagraj Ghat Tak
17. Yatra Ranjendra Prasad Ghat se Dattatreya Ghat Tak
18. YaatraSindhiya Ghat se Gwaliar Ghat Tak
19. Yatra Mangala Gauri Ghat se Hanuman Gadhi Ghat Tak
20. Yatra Gaay Ghat Se Nishad Ghat Tak
21. MAA GANGA, GHATEN EVM UTSAV
22. Ganga Arti Dev Deepavali evam Any Utsav
23. Potentials of Digitalized India
24. VEDIC CONSCIOUSNESS
25. A Brief Introduction to Vedic Science
26. Kashi ke Barah Jyotirling
27. IMPACT OF MOTIVATION
28. Let's have a Milky Way Journey
29. Color Therapy in a Nutshell

30. Rigveda in a Nutshell
31. Yajurveda in a Nutshell
32. Samveda in a Nutshell
33. Atharva Veda in a Nutshell
34. Ayushman Bhava - Ayurveda
35. Srimad Bhagavad Gita and Upanishad Connection
36. Srimad Bhagavad Gita - an attempt to summarize each chapter.
37. Facts and Impact of Nakshatra
38. Astro Gems - NAVARATNA
39. Ekadashi - A Concise Overview
40. A Concise View of Hanuman Chalisa
41. Inspirational Gita
42. Nakshatraranyam
43. Summary of 18 Mahapuranas
44. Synopsis of 18 Upa Puranas
45. Rigvediya Upanishads
46. Shukla Yajurvediya Upanishads
47. Krishna Yajurvediya Upanishads
48. Samavediya Upanishads
49. Atharvavediya Upanishads
50. The Seven Great Sages
51. From Rocket Scientist to President Dr. APJ Abdul Kalam
52. The Visionary's Voice - Quotes of Dr. APJ Abdul Kalam
53. The Wisdom of Swami Vivekananda: Insights and Inspiration from a Legendary Spiritual Teacher
54. Ayurvedic Remedies from the Garden
55. Sages and Seers
56. Rising Strong – Motivational Stories of Women
57. Beyond Flames -Mystery stories of Funeral Ghat Manikarnika
58. The Origins of Tulsi: A Look at the Mythological Roots of the Plant"

ϷϷϷ

Contact

DR. JAGADEESH PILLAI

PhD in Vedic Science

Four Times Guinness World Record Holder

Winner of Mahatma Gandhi Vishwa Shanti Puraskar and
Global Peace Ambassador

Gemology, Astro & Vastu Consultant - Spiritual Counselor

Consultant for designing World Record Ideas

Efficient Tarot Card Reader

9839093003

myrichindia@gmail.com

drjagadeeshpillai@facebook

drjagadeeshpillai@instagram

jagadeeshpillai@youtube

www. JAGADEESHPILLAI.com

ϼϼϼ

|| LOKAHA SAMASTHAHA SUKHINO BHAVANTU ||

• 67 •

* 9 7 9 8 8 8 9 5 1 0 9 1 8 *